NATIONAL GEOGRAPHIC

Watermelons

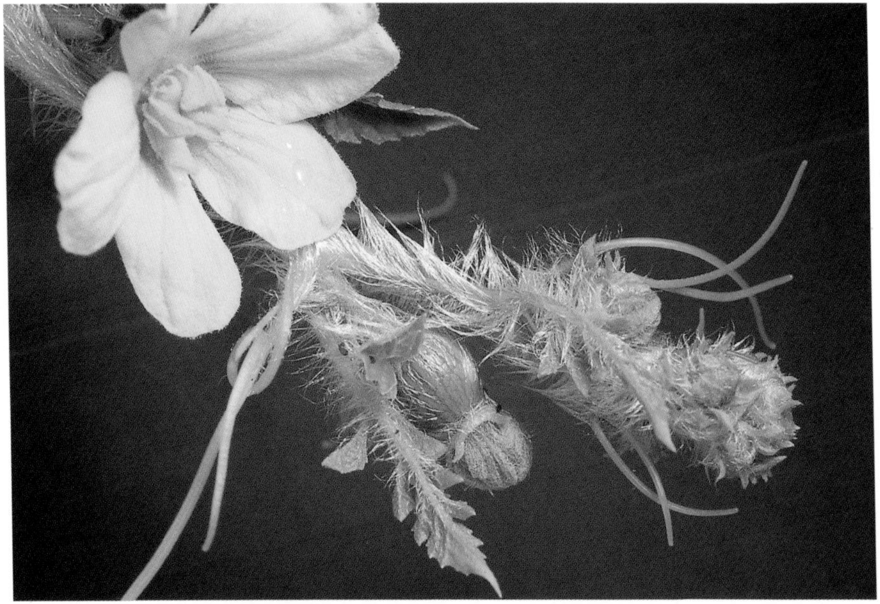

Terry O'Brady

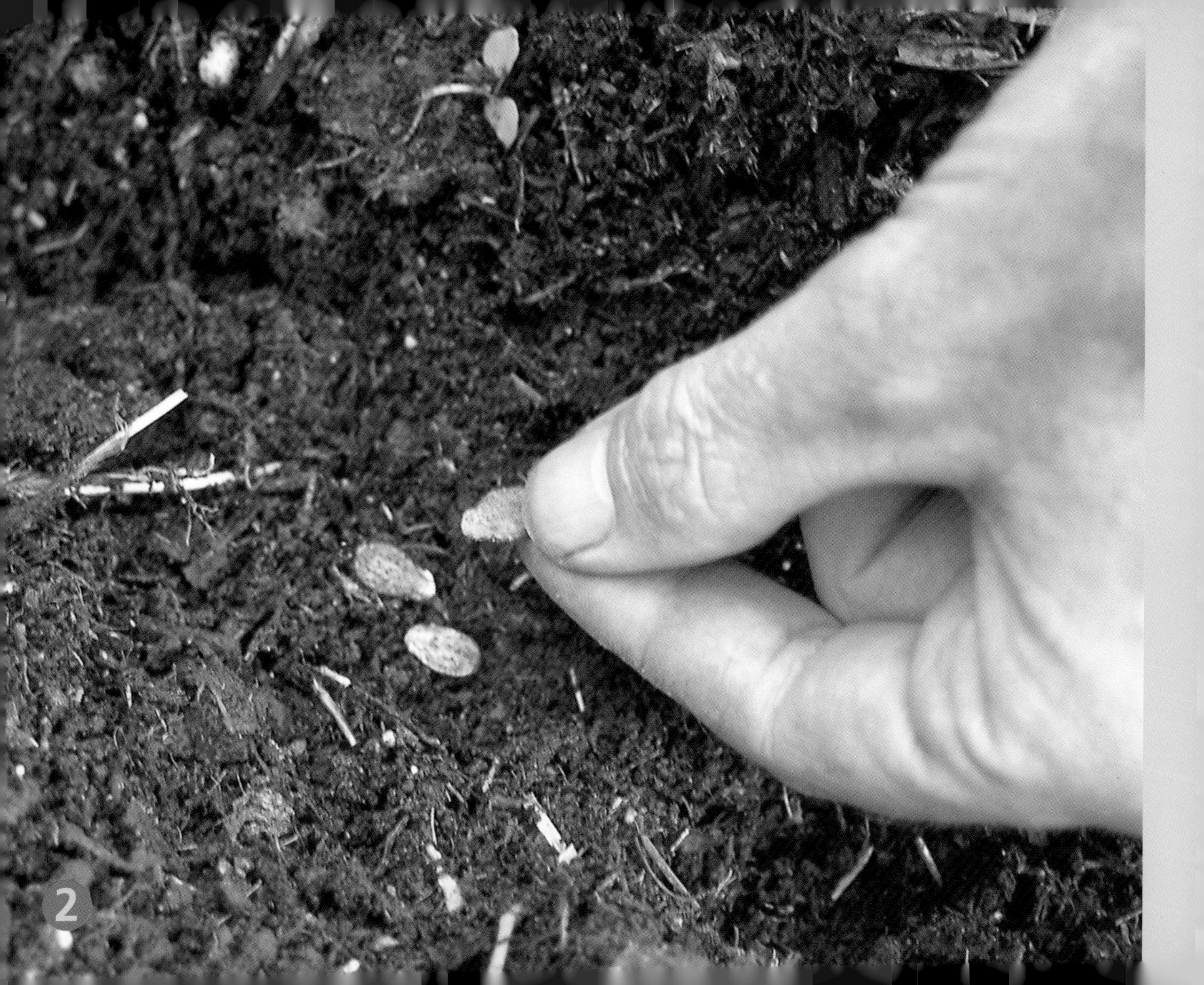
2

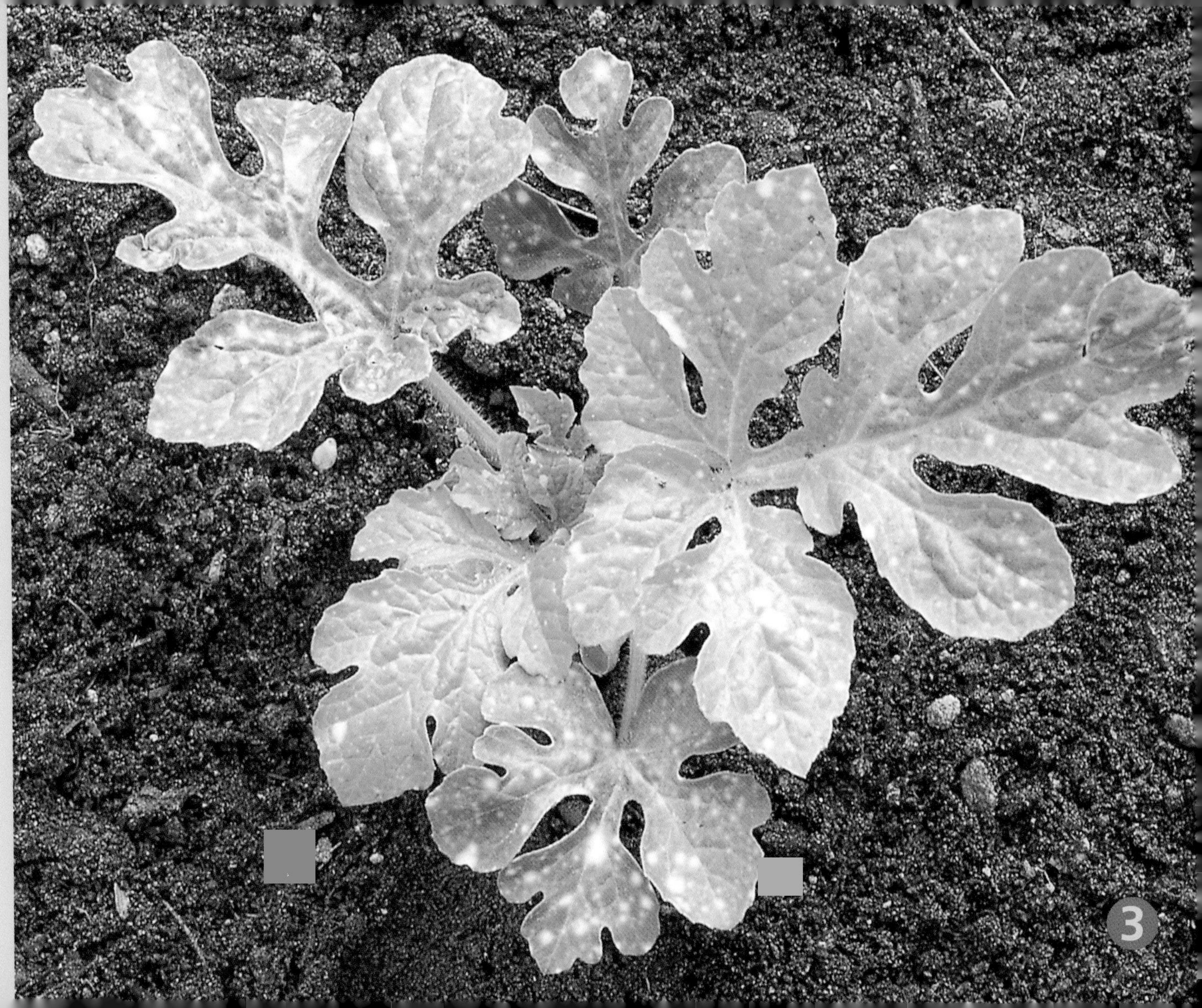
3

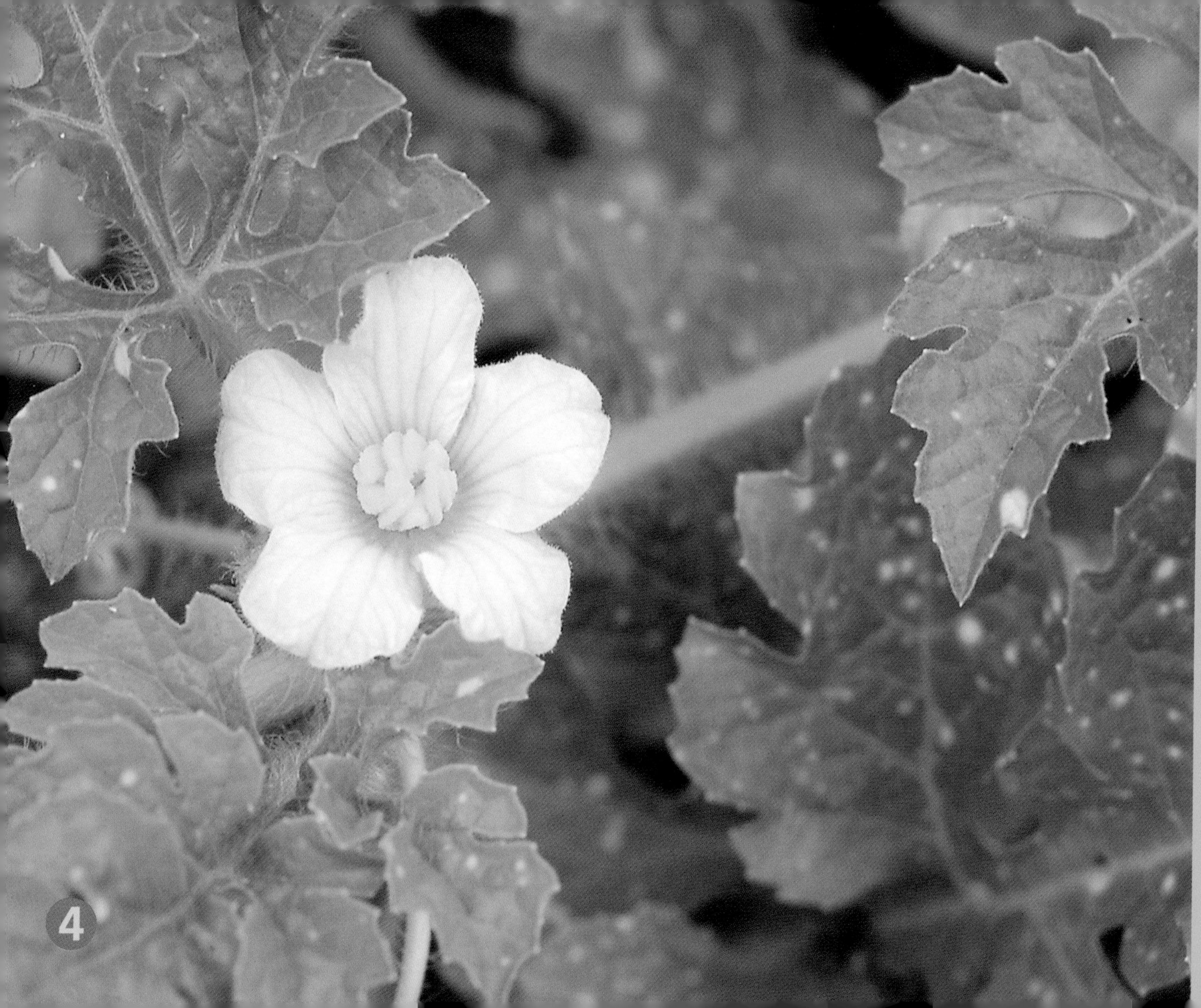
4

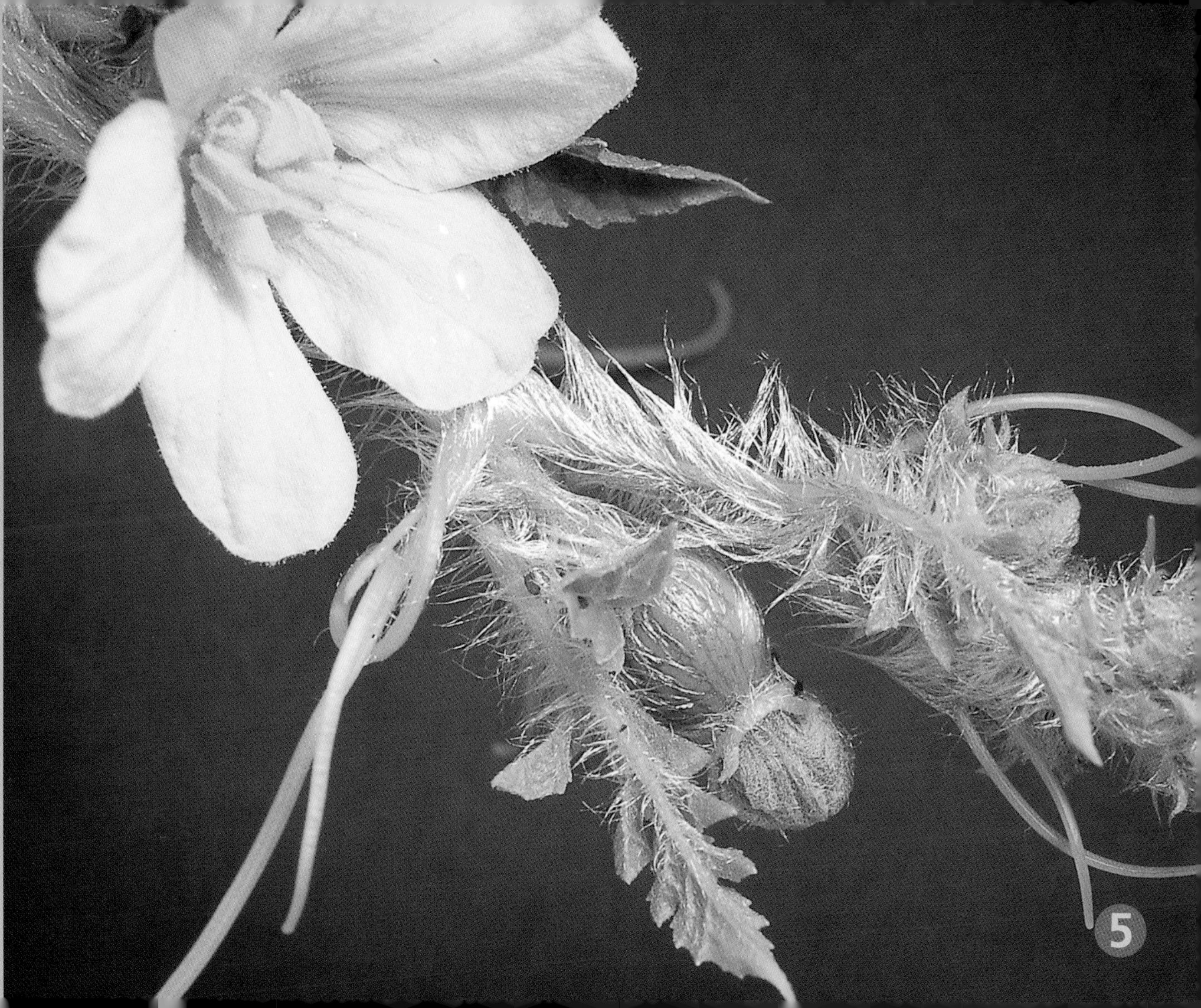
5

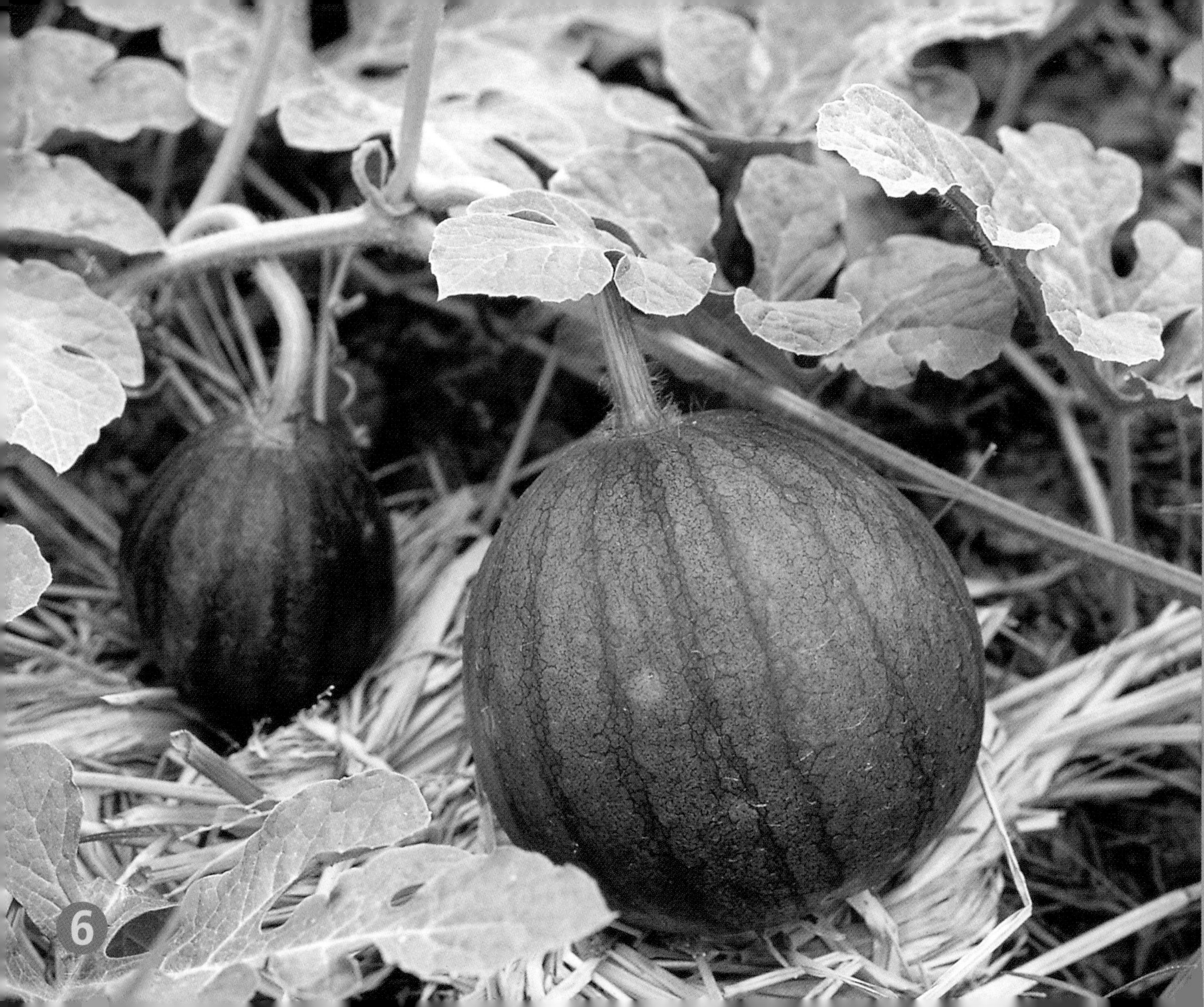
6

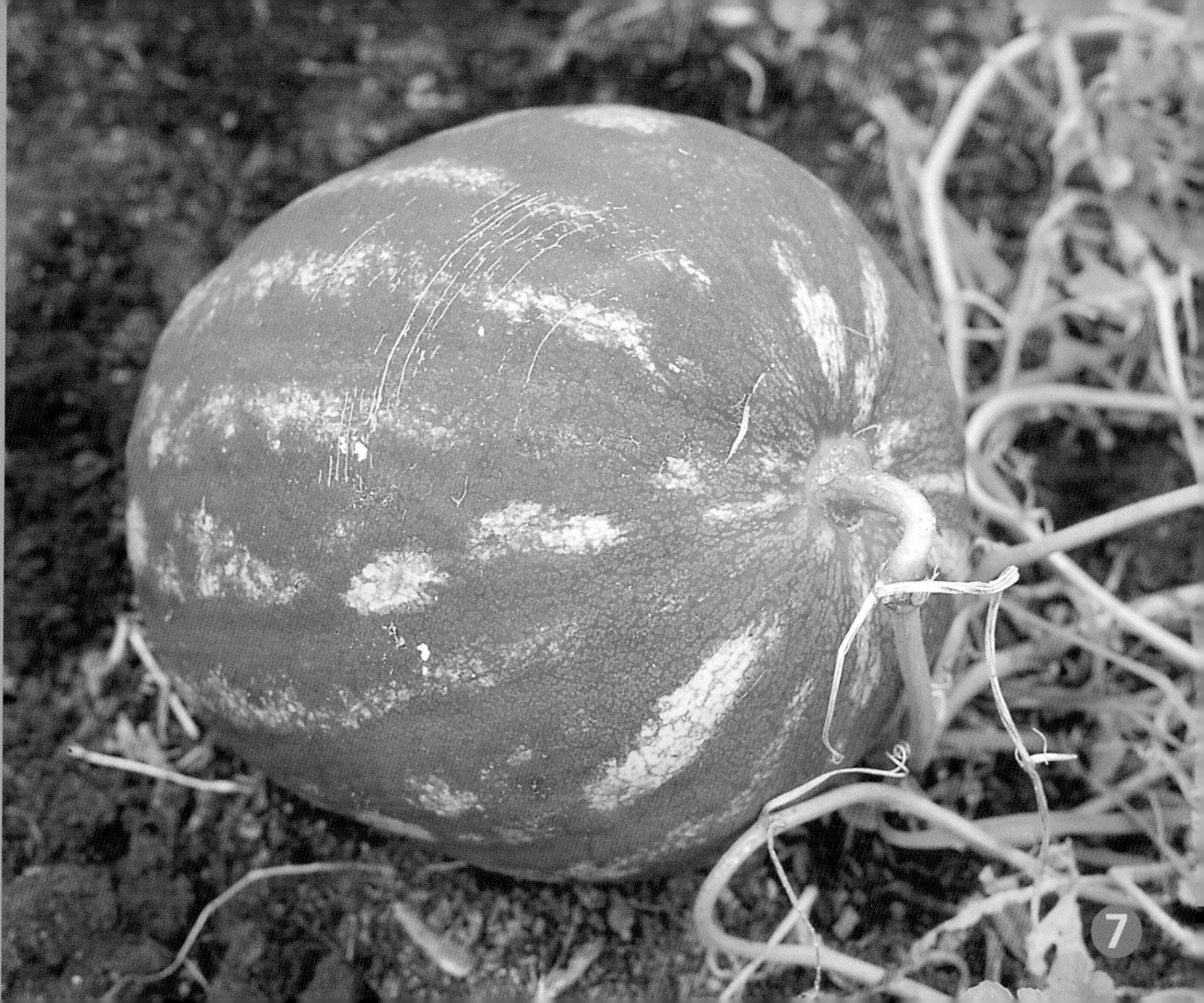

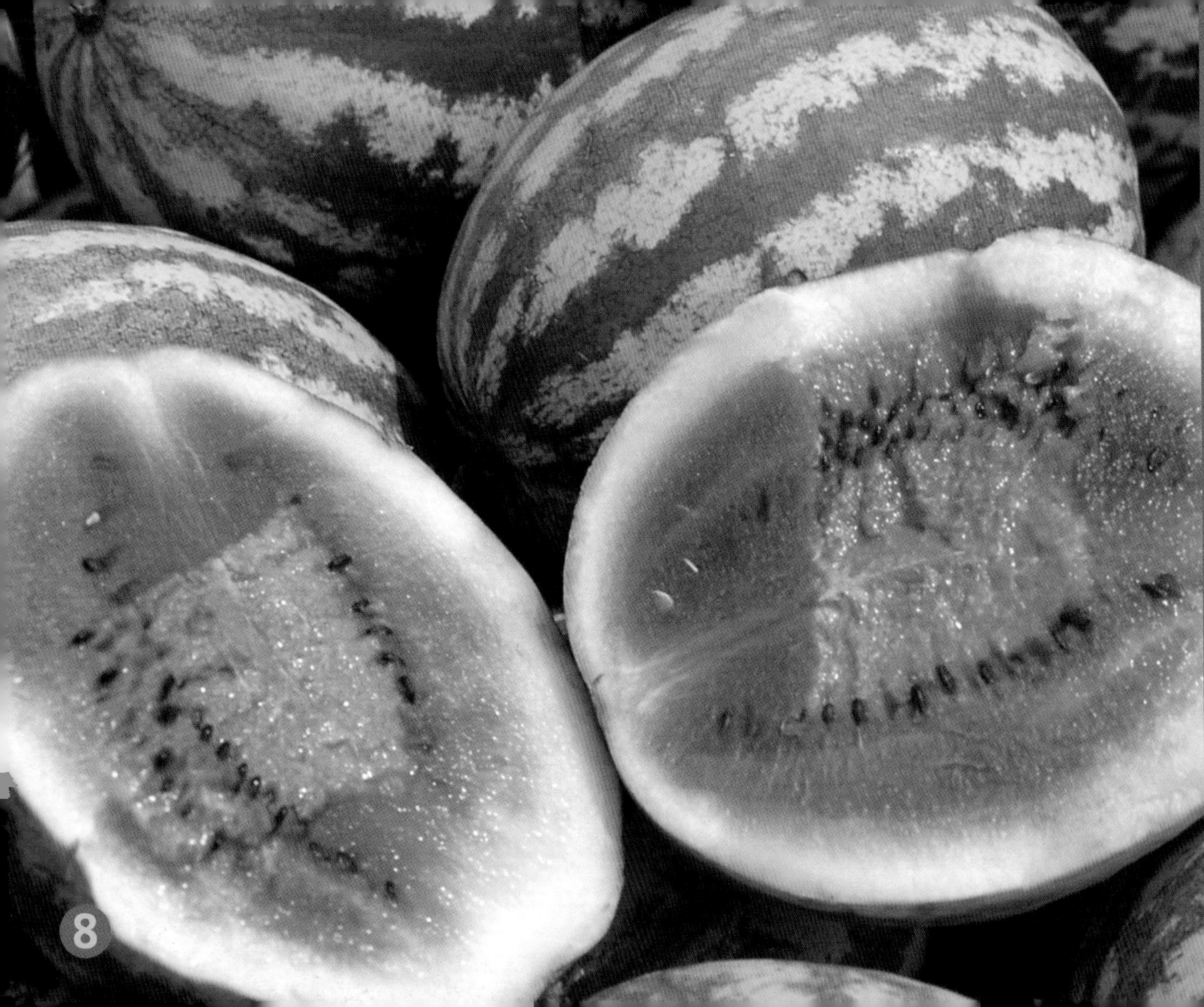